# THE P.A.T.C.H PARABLE

## A STORY ABOUT LEAKS, LESSONS, AND LASTING CHANGE

DANIEL JARVIS

Copyright Page

P.A.T.C.H

# DEDICATION

To my brother Joseph Jarvis —
   our long talks about growth and leadership
   were basically a podcast no one recorded.
   This book is the closest we'll get.

# ABOUT THE AUTHOR

My name is Daniel Jarvis, and I am a registered dietitian, Air Force veteran. I've always been drawn to movement — strength training, running, swimming, rowing, HIIT, anything that makes the heart beat faster and reminds you that you're alive. I'm also the former co-race director of the Kanawha Trace 50k/25k/10k and the Moonlight Madness/Darkness Falls night trail races.

Throughout my life, I've learned best through acronyms, analogies, stories, and doing the work myself. I teach the same way — through parables, simple frameworks, and lessons that stick. I believe in making things just difficult enough that you don't want to do them at first, because that's how growth works. What starts out hard eventually becomes easy, and when it does, you pause, reflect, reanalyze, and take action again.

Motivation always runs out. Discipline is what carries you forward. I've learned that after three to four months of pushing, the body and mind need a reset —

just a week or two — and then you return stronger. This rhythm helps break plateaus in fitness, work, and life.

The P.A.T.C.H. Parable comes from that same philosophy. It blends my favorite topics: amygdala hijacks, pausing before reacting, reflecting honestly, analyzing what you're capable of right now, and focusing on what you can do in this moment. Then, when the time is right, you build on it.

My hope is that this parable helps you recognize your own leaks, repair them with intention, and move forward with clarity and confidence.

# INTRODUCTION

This parable is about Sam and his journey to lose weight, gain muscle, become a trail runner, write poetry, learn to play the guitar, manage his job, take care of his family, and stay connected with his friends. Sam wants to improve every part of his life at the same time. So, he does what most of us do — he tries to change everything at once. And just like most of us, he gives up after a few weeks.

Every January 1st, he starts again. Every February, he fades out. He lives in the shadows of his goals, always trying, always restarting, never getting anywhere. Not because he's lazy. Not because he doesn't care. But because he's taking on too much at once. Sam doesn't know it yet, but his bucket is full of holes.

Every time he fills it with effort — new habits, new

routines, new goals — the water leaks out. His motivation drains. His energy drains. His confidence drains. Eventually the bucket is empty, and he quits.

When you have a bucket full of holes, you have two choices: get a new bucket, or patch the holes. You can't erase yourself and start over. But you can work with yourself. You can repair what's leaking.

One day, while hiking through the woods, Sam notices an old metal bucket hanging from a wooden sign. The bucket is full of holes, and carved into the sign are the words: "Gene was here." Inside the bucket is a stack of laminated pamphlets with a simple message:

**P.A.T.C.H.** the holes in your bucket one at a time.

- **P** — Pause and identify the leaks
- **A** — Accept the challenge
- **T** — Tackle it one step at a time
- **C** — Create a plan you can stick to
- **H** — Hang up the bucket and examine it

Sam takes a pamphlet and continues down the trail, not realizing that this small moment is the beginning of every real transformation: understanding your root causes. Before you can change your life, you have to understand why it keeps leaking.

## 1

### SEEING THE REAL PROBLEM

Sam was invited to go on a trail run out at the Boy Scout Camp by one of his friends. Just a simple six-mile loop that circled the entire camp — a mix of the Kanawha Trace, the Adahi Trail, and a two-mile road section. Nothing crazy. Nothing he hadn't thought about doing before.

He drove out to the camp and met his friend at their usual spot. Sometimes they met inside the gate, sometimes outside — it all depended on whether camp was in session. Today, the place was quiet. Perfect running weather.

They took off down the river trail first, starting faster than Sam expected. His friend let him go ahead, laughing under his breath. Sam didn't know why until he ran face-first into the first cobweb.

Then the second. Then the third. His friend burst out laughing. "I needed a cobweb clearer," he said between breaths. "One of the perks of inviting people to run with me."

Sam wiped his face, groaned, and grabbed a stick off the ground. He held it out in front of him like a sword as he ran. His friend laughed even harder. "Fast learner. Took you less than a minute."

They left the river trail and hit the long road section, settling into a steady rhythm. They crossed the Big Cabell Creek bridge, climbed toward Fat Man's Misery, pushed up toward Adams Hollow, and worked their way across two big hills.

And at the top of the second hill, Sam saw it. A bucket. An old metal bucket full of holes, hanging from a weathered wooden sign that read: GENE WAS HERE

Sam slowed to a walk. Something about it pulled him in — the way it swayed slightly in the breeze, the way the sunlight hit the rusted metal, the way it felt like it was waiting for him. Inside the bucket was a laminated flyer. He reached in and pulled it out.

It read:

**P.A.T.C.H.** the holes in your bucket one at a time.

- **P** — Pause and identify the leaks
- **A** — Accept the challenge
- **T** — Tackle it one step at a time

- **C** — Create a plan you can stick to
- **H** — Hang up the bucket and examine it

Sam stared at it longer than he meant to. Something about it felt... personal. Like it was meant for him. Like the woods themselves had handed him a message.

He folded the flyer carefully, tucked it into his pocket, and jogged to catch up with his friend. When they finished the loop, Sam washed the cobwebs off his face at the spigot, checked for ticks, said goodbye, and headed home. He didn't know it yet, but that bucket was about to change everything.

Sam wakes up every day feeling stuck. He stands in front of the mirror and barely recognizes the man staring back at him. It's not just the way he looks — it's the weight of everything he hasn't become. He feels like he's falling short of his own life goals, drifting through a fog of unfinished dreams.

His mind wanders through a lifetime of attempts: some wins, but mostly a long trail of goals he started and never finished. Losing weight. Gaining muscle. Writing poetry. Becoming a trail runner. Learning to play the guitar. Managing the demands of his job. Taking care of his family. Staying connected to his friends. All good intentions, all half-built bridges.

Every year, he makes a list. Every January 1st, he starts again. Dieting. Going to the gym. Practicing the guitar. Showing up at work. Trying to be a good husband, a good father, a good friend — all at the same time. And every year, the same thing happens: he burns out, fades out, and falls back into the shadows of the life he wants but can't seem to reach.

Sam thinks back to an unfinished poem. Several years ago, he wanted to run the Kanawha Trace Darkness Falls Haunted Trail Run. He talked about it for weeks, hyped himself up, imagined the headlamps glowing through the trees... and then he never signed up. Just another goal he let slip through the cracks.

He had even started writing a poem about the race — something fun, something spooky, something that captured the thrill he hoped to feel. But like everything else in his life, he never finished it. His days were full of leaking holes, and his bucket was spilling water everywhere.

All he had left were the last few lines:

Dust off your headlamps and follow the glow!

It's dark and spooky in the woods just so you know!

Lace up your trail shoes nice and tight!

Be cautious and vigilant and watch for the fright!

He looked at the unfinished poem and sighed.

Gosh... I never finish anything.

His bucket was so full of holes he could practically hear the water dripping out. That thought led him straight to another leak — the guitar.

He remembered how excited he'd been. He went to the music store, held every guitar in the place, picked the one that felt right in his hands. He bought a beginner's book, brought it home, learned how to tune it… and then leaned it against the wall, where it stayed. Days passed. Weeks. Months. Years. Now he walked by it like it was a ghost of the person he wanted to be. Just another hole in the bucket.

And while he was thinking about holes in buckets, a memory bubbled up from elementary school music class — that old song they used to sing:

There's a hole in the bucket, dear Georgy…

With what shall I fill it, dear Liza…

He couldn't remember the whole thing, just the rhythm of it, the way the class would laugh as they sang it. But now, standing in the middle of his messy life, the meaning hit him differently.

Georgy and Liza were trying to fill a leaky bucket too. And here he was, decades later, living the same song. My life is a bucket full of holes, he thought. Just like theirs.

Sam then moved on to the next set of holes — the ones that hurt the most. Being a good father. Being a good husband. Being a good friend.

He always showed up to work on time. He always took his kids where they needed to go — practices, games, school events, last-minute errands. He always answered texts from friends, checked in, kept the conversations alive. On the outside, he looked dependable. Solid. Responsible.

But the moment he tried to add anything for himself — poetry, guitar, trail running, dieting, strength training — everything fell apart.

He would start dieting and do well for a while… until the road trips came. Until the temptations at volleyball, cheer, and basketball tournaments. Until the long days, the late nights, the concession stands, the gas-station snacks, the "we'll just grab something quick" moments.

He'd try to meal prep, but then he'd run short on time on the way to work. Fast food again. He'd try to get to the gym, but then everything else would fall behind. He'd try to run, but then he'd be too tired to do anything else. Every time he tried to put it all together, something slipped. Then another thing. Then everything.

Sam wasn't failing because he didn't care. He was failing because his bucket was leaking faster than he could fill it. Now that Sam has identified his leaks he is ready to accept the challenge and own the work ahead.

2
———

# OWNING THE WORK AHEAD

Sam knew the road ahead was going to be rough. He had a lot of holes to patch, and for the first time in his life, he didn't run from that truth. He just sat with it. Letting the idea roast. Letting it settle into his bones.

He thought about how many times he had tried to write poetry and quit before he was finished. He remembered visualizing the Darkness Falls night race — the campfire, the s'mores, the people dressed up as scarers. He remembered hearing about the hot apple cider and the soups at the finish line. Not just any soups, either. Chili. Vegetarian chili. Burgoo with real bourbon. Potato soup. Cream of tomato. The prepackaged s'more kits. The cannon fire that started the race. The glowsticks lining the trail. The hours of work it took to snap them and set them out. The headlamps flicking on. The runners lining up. The blast of the cannon. The three scare zones. The chicken route for the faint of heart. The homemade wooden medals for the top finishers.

He held all of that in his mind — the sights, the smells, the sounds — and tucked it away like a spark he could return to later. When he was ready, he'd pull it back out and use it to finish his poem.

He heard countless stories from others who had run it, and this is what he remembered; there is nothing in the world like the feeling of turning on your headlamp and heading out for a trail run that has been marked so you don't get lost. The spookiness of the woods at night. The fake glowing eyes on the river trail. The real glowing eyes of the deer and squirrels and whatever else is out there watching you from the woods. Old Baldy lurking somewhere in the dark, or at least in your imagination. The way the trail feels different at night — quieter, louder, heavier, lighter — all at the same time.

The view of trail runners going down the switchbacks when the leaves have fallen off the trees, and you can see nothing but silhouettes of runners' lights trailing down the hill like a glowing river. The feeling when your headlamp dies out and you are truly alone in the dark. Your eyes adjusting slowly, your breath getting louder, your heartbeat sounding like footsteps behind you. You follow the glowsticks because that's all you have. You run faster because something in the woods always feels like it's running with you.

There's just something that spooks you when you're running at night in the woods with nothing but other runners somewhere out there and the sound of your own breathing. The hills, the sweat, the scarers don't even scare you — you know they're just people in costumes. It's the critters that get you. The unknown. The things that could be watching. You know the scarers can't touch you, but the animals? That's a mystery. Old Baldy — is he real? What was that sound? Was it another runner? A deer? A coyote? A panther? Gene? What is it? Your mind plays tricks on you, and your legs do the rest.

Finally, you finish up by the campfire and the smell hits you — soup, hot apple cider, hot chocolate, s'mores, hot dogs. Just your regular campfire atmosphere but somehow better because you earned it. And if you're lucky, you're a 1, 2, or 3 and you get a medal. A real wooden medal. Handmade. Something you can't buy, only earn.

It was everything Sam loved about trail running. Everything he missed. Everything he wanted to feel again. And all of it — every smell, every sound, every flicker of light — went into the mental vault he kept for the day he would finally finish his poem.

I've got this, he told himself. Then he thought about the next leak: trail running. He knew the first two or three weeks were always the hardest. He remembered how strength training made running easier. So he made a plan — start with hiking and strength training, then slowly add running back in. Break in slowly. Reduce the DOMS. Build the habit without burning out. I'm going to own this, he said.

Next on his list was the guitar. He realized he'd been thinking about it all wrong. He didn't need to magically teach himself. He needed lessons. Maybe thirty minutes a month. Something small. Something doable. He'd go back to the music store and ask about options.

The rest — being there for his family, his friends, his job — that part came naturally. That wasn't the problem. That wasn't where the leaks were.

So Sam made a decision. A quiet one. A steady one. He was going to own this. One leak at a time. One patch at a time. One step at a time. And for the first time in a long time, he put his best foot forward.

Sam thought back to why he loved trail running so much. It wasn't just the races or the medals or the stories people told afterward. It was the woods themselves — the calm, the quiet, the peace that wrapped around you the moment you stepped off the pavement and onto dirt. The woods didn't judge you. They didn't rush you. They didn't demand anything from you. They just let you be.

You could go there and release all the stress of the day. You could be alone without being lonely. You could let the tension drain out of your shoulders with every footstep. You could breathe deeper. Think clearer. Feel lighter. The woods had a way of pulling the truth out of you — the feelings you kept inside, the frustrations you swallowed, the worries you carried around like stones in your pockets. Out there, you could finally let them go.

Trail running had always been one of his vices — one of the good ones. One of the ways he used to chase that feel-good rush from the endorphins. He knew the endorphins didn't last forever. They were short-lived, a spark that faded after a few hours. But the woods... the woods had their own kind of magic. Their own mystery. Their own way of connecting you to something bigger than yourself. When you were out there, surrounded by trees and dirt and wind and silence, all in the world felt okay — at least for the time you were in the woods.

He knew getting back to that would be good for him. Good for his work. Good for his family. Good for the version of himself he wanted to become. He needed a place to let the negativity go — to let it fall away with each footstep, each deep breath, each lungful of fresh forest air. The woods had always been that place. A reset button. A release valve. A reminder that he was still alive, still capable, still connected to something real.

And he missed it. He missed it more than he realized. Sam thought about the guitar next. His friend was incredible at it — the kind of player who made it look effortless. But Sam knew the truth behind it. His friend didn't just wake up one day with talent. He took lessons. He practiced for hours. He collected guitars the way some people collected memories — ten, maybe fifteen of them, plus drums and amps and pedals and everything else you could imagine. Music was his world.

Sam knew he didn't have that kind of time. He didn't have hours to dedicate to anything. But he did have a few minutes a day. Or a few minutes a week. Enough to learn something. Enough to make progress. Enough to feel like he wasn't abandoning himself again.

He didn't need fifteen guitars. He didn't need a studio. He didn't need the hype. He just needed one guitar, his fingers, a tuner, and a willingness to learn the basics — the ABCDEFG, the minors and majors, where to place his fingers, how to strum, when to pick, how to read music, how to build rhythm, how to strengthen his hands, how to hold the guitar without feeling awkward. He needed all of that, and he knew it.

Right now, he only had the guitar, a few picks, a tuner, and a faded memory of wanting something more.

But if he could learn — even slowly — he might be able to take one of his poems and turn it into a song. Something simple. Something honest. Something he could play around a campfire someday.

Then his mind drifted to the road trips — baseball, softball, cheer. Endless weekends of driving, hotels, concession stands, and fast food. It was a lot. A whole lot. But there was downtime too. More than he admitted. He knew he could make better choices if he really wanted to. You could eat healthy on the road if you planned ahead. You could use the hotel kitchen. You could buy groceries instead of grabbing whatever was closest. It wasn't easy, but it was possible.

You could go for walks or runs outside the hotel if you picked the right spot. You could temporarily use the treadmill — the "dreadmill," as he called it — even though he hated it. And during the downtime, he could write poems. He could work on a song. He could read about guitar chords. He could learn something small. He could grow in tiny ways. And he could still spend time with his family. Still go out to eat. Still enjoy the break from work and the chaos of everyday life. He didn't need perfection. He just needed intention.

And just because he was in the moment — really in it — Sam surprised himself. He picked up his notebook, stared at the first four lines of the poem he'd abandoned years ago, and before he even realized what was happening, the next four lines spilled out of him. It wasn't finished. Not even close. But it was progress. Real progress. The kind he hadn't felt in years.

He looked down at what he had now — eight lines, marked out in his handwriting, alive again after sitting dormant for so long:

Dust off your headlamps and follow the glow!

It's dark and spooky in the woods just so you know!

Lace up your trail shoes nice and tight!

Be cautious and vigilant and watch for the fright!

Into the woods you will eventually go!

Just follow the light and go with the flow!

Up and down the hills you will flee!

Turn off your lights just for a second to see!

He read them twice.Then a third time. They weren't perfect. They weren't polished. But they were his.

And for the first time in a long time, Sam felt something shift inside him — a tiny spark, a flicker of the person he used to be. The person he still wanted to become. Eight lines. A start. A patch on one of his leaks.

Sam closed his notebook and let out a long breath. Eight lines. A spark. A start. It wasn't everything, but it was something — and something was more than he'd had in years. For the first time, he felt like he wasn't just identifying the leaks in his bucket. He was actually doing something about them.

And that was the moment he realized the truth:

patching a bucket doesn't happen all at once. It happens slowly. Deliberately. One leak at a time.

He looked at the **P.A.T.C.H.** flyer again, his eyes landing on the next step.

T — Tackle it one step at a time.

He wasn't ready to fix everything. But he was ready to fix something. And that was enough to begin.

3

---

## SMALL WINS, BIG MOMENTUM

Before Sam could get to work, he stopped to think — or at least he tried to. That was when his dog came barreling around the corner, tail wagging like a helicopter blade, and slammed into him with a full-body lean. Muddy paws everywhere. Sam laughed despite himself and let the dog climb all over him, rubbing its dirty paws across his shirt like it was signing its name.

He played with the dog for a minute, letting the moment pull him out of his head. Then the dog finally settled, flopped down at his feet, and looked up at him with that expectant "Well? What now?" expression.

Sam smiled. He pawsed. And in that quiet little pause — muddy shirt, happy dog, breath slowing — he thought about the next step.

Tackle it one step at a time. He wiped the muddy paw prints off his shirt and smirked. Pawsing was a sign of intelligence, he told himself. Well... as long as you could spell pause correctly.

Before Sam laced up for his first trail run, he paused and let his mind drift back to where it all began. Years ago, Danny and Joey had invited him to tag along for the WV Trilogy weekend. They ran the 50K on Friday, then stayed to volunteer for the 50-miler the next day — the kind of thing only trail runners think is normal.

They brought a giant pot of burgoo, the same recipe the Orange Blur had sworn would change lives at the night races. And he wasn't wrong. By the time runners staggered into Mile 20, cold and cracked open by the mountains, that burgoo was a miracle in a bowl. Sam spent the day ladling it out, watching people come back to life one steaming cup at a time.

He remembered the gratitude in their eyes, the way they leaned on the table, the way they laughed through the pain. He remembered cheering Danny and Joey across the finish line, muddy and exhausted and grinning like idiots. And he remembered the whole weekend — camping in a tent, eating breakfast and dinner in a yurt, watching runners complete a 50K, then a 50-miler, then a half marathon like it was nothing.

It left him in awe. That was the moment trail running hooked him, not the running itself, but the community, the grit, the way people came alive out there.

And now, years later, he felt that spark again. He woke up ready. Ready to run. Ready to return to the thing that once made him feel like he belonged. He had already signed up for the night race in October. This was his first step back.

Sam decided the next hole he needed to patch was the guitar. Trail running could wait a little longer — the mountains weren't going anywhere — but this? This was something he could start today. Something small. Something doable.

So he signed up for lessons. One thirty-minute session a week. Nothing overwhelming. Nothing heroic. Just a commitment he could keep. And he promised himself he'd practice ten minutes a day. Ten minutes wasn't scary. Ten minutes was a step.

Since trail running had always been his thing, he searched online for a song that matched the feeling of being out there — the rhythm, the movement, the forward momentum. He landed on "Running on Empty" by Jackson Browne. The title alone felt like it understood him. It was the soundtrack of every long run he'd ever done, every moment he'd pushed past what he thought he had left.

But before he could get anywhere near that song, he had to learn the basics. His first lesson wasn't glamorous — just chords. Finger positions. Awkward shapes. Buzzing strings. The kind of beginning that humbles you fast.

Still, it was a start. A small win. And for the first time in a long time, Sam felt like he wasn't running on empty anymore. He was filling the tank, one tiny step at a time.

Sam got out his guitar and strummed a few notes that were absolutely, undeniably out of tune. He winced, laughed, and tried again. This time he found the G chord. Then the D. Then the A. His fingers felt stiff and clumsy, but he kept going, cycling through the sequence like his teacher showed him.

G twice. A once. Back to D. Repeat. Slow at first. Then a little smoother. Then smoother still. Before long he was tapping his foot, trying to find a rhythm that felt like something. He was grooving — in his own crooked, beginner way. He was strumming. He was picking. He was making music. It had no script. It had no structure. It had no real direction. It was just... spontaneous. Alive. His.

And for the first time in a long time, Sam felt something shift inside him. Not a big shift. Not a dramatic breakthrough. Just a tiny, steady drip of progress.His hole — this old, neglected, dusty guitar-shaped hole — was being slowly patched. One chord at a time.

As Sam set the guitar down for a moment, he

thought about his poem — the one he'd finally added four new lines to after all these years. It surprised him how good it felt to make progress on something he'd abandoned for so long. And that progress stirred up old memories he hadn't visited in decades.

He remembered being a kid on the school bus, staring out the window while words and rhythms just... appeared. Lines of poetry. Snippets of melodies. Little sparks of something he didn't have a name for yet. His mind moved faster than his hands ever could, and back then, writing meant a pencil, a notebook, and a race he always lost. Computers weren't much help either — unless you counted playing Oregon Trail on the old Apple machines, which every kid did and none of them regretted.

His hand couldn't keep up with his imagination. But the spark was there. It wasn't until he got older — until he learned to type, until he got his first real computer — that he realized he actually liked writing. That he could finally keep pace with the ideas that used to outrun him.

He remembered the first poem he ever wrote. He was eighteen, in love for the first time, and the words poured out of him like they'd been waiting years to escape:

"Remembering the bliss and all the specialness,

to what extent do I love, my love is so far and above.

The light from her eyes fills the sunshine in the skies,

the rosiness of her cheeks will always reach the highest mountain peaks.

Listen to me my dear, there is nothing to fear.

Something worth saying never should be mistaken for playing.

Let the sands of time become intertwine

with the strong feelings of love from my mind."

He smiled at the memory — not because the poem was perfect, but because it was him. Raw. Honest. Young. Trying. And remembering it now lit something inside him. A spark. A push.

A reminder that he'd always been a creator, even when he didn't know how to capture the things swirling in his head. He felt motivated. He felt alive. He felt ready. October was coming. The Darkness Falls night race was waiting. And so was the last line of his poem. Sam was ready to run again — and ready to finish what he started.

Before Sam could run, he knew he needed to get stronger. Not bodybuilder strong — just trail-runner strong. The kind of strength that keeps your knees from buckling on downhills and your lungs from quitting on the climbs.

He thought back to high school weight-training class, where "lifting" basically meant bench press and bicep curls. That was the whole curriculum. Nobody talked about deadlifts or squats or shoulder presses. Nobody explained how to build a foundation. He'd learned just enough to feel like he should know more, but not enough to actually get fit.

Now, standing in the present, he realized how much he still had to learn — and how much he'd avoided learning because it felt overwhelming. But this time was different. This time he wasn't trying to overhaul his life in a day. Tackle it one step at a time. He didn't need a perfect program. He didn't need four sets of everything. He didn't need to max out or chase numbers. He just needed to show up. One or two sets with light weights.

Build to three. Then maybe four. Ease into it so he didn't get crushed by DOMS and lose two days to soreness. More than he was doing now was better than nothing — and "better than nothing" was a win. Sam felt a quiet confidence settle in. He didn't have to be an expert. He just had to begin.

Even with all the leaks Sam was trying to patch, he knew there were parts of his life that were solid. Work, for example — that wasn't a hole. He showed up, did his job, and did it well. His reviews were always strong, sometimes exceeding expectations, sometimes meeting them, but never dipping below the line. He got kudos, recognition, the occasional "nice job" email that reminded him he wasn't failing everywhere.

And his family — that wasn't a hole either. He took his kids to practice, to games, to school events. He did the dad stuff. The real dad stuff. The everyday, unglamorous, consistent things that mattered more than he ever gave himself credit for.

Then there were his friends. The group chats. The check-ins. The way each friend required a different version of him — one needed jokes, one needed honesty, one needed encouragement, one needed space. Sam kept up with all of them, one by one, because that's who he was. He didn't always say the perfect thing, but he showed up. And showing up counted.

These weren't holes. These were strengths. These were the parts of his life that were already patched, already holding steady. And realizing that gave him something he hadn't felt in a long time — confidence. Not the loud kind. Not the chest-puffed-out kind.

Just a quiet, steady belief that he wasn't starting from zero. He had a foundation. He had things he was already doing right. And that meant he could build from here.

Sam sat in his room with the guitar resting across his lap and the computer screen glowing in front of him. He bounced between strumming a few chords, typing out lines of poems, and jotting down short story ideas as they drifted through his mind. For the first time in a long time, his creative energy felt awake — not forced, not frantic, just quietly alive.

He thought about running. He thought about lifting. He thought about the guitar. He thought about how good his life already was — work steady, family strong, friendships intact. He didn't need to rebuild everything. He just had a few holes to patch, and none of them needed to be fixed overnight.

The universe had its own timeline. And for once, Sam wasn't trying to outrun it. He was taking the first steps — small, steady, intentional. Steps toward whatever the universe had in store for him next. Steps toward becoming the version of himself he'd always felt flickering beneath the surface.

He didn't know exactly where it would lead. But he knew this much: It was time to make a plan.

4

———

## NO MORE FANTASY PLANS

Sam remembered reading once that a vision board could help keep your goals in front of you — not as decoration, but as a daily reminder of who you're trying to become. So he drove to the store and picked up a white dry-erase board, a pack of markers, and a stack of note cards with a few pencils and pens. If he was going to change his life, he wanted three different ways to see it: written, visual, and tangible.

When he got home, he set the board on the table and drew three columns across the top:

Start — Now — Future Self

He stared at the "Start" column for a long moment, then wrote the only four things that mattered:

- Running
- Weight Training
- Guitar
- Poetry

Those were his leaks. Those were his holes. Those were the things he kept abandoning. The "Now" column stayed empty — because today, "now" was the same as "start." He wrote the date underneath it, a quiet acknowledgment of where he stood.

Then he moved to the "Future Self" column and wrote out the version of him he wanted to grow into:

- Run 3–5 days per week
- Weight train every other day
- Finish the poem and brainstorm 5 minutes a day
- Play guitar 10 minutes a day and take weekly lessons

When he finished, he stepped back and looked at the board. It wasn't fancy. It wasn't artistic. It wasn't something you'd post online for likes. But it was honest. It was him.

He picked up the board, walked to the hallway, and hung it where he'd have to see it every single day — the place where excuses couldn't hide and old habits couldn't sneak back in.

For the first time in a long time, Sam felt like he wasn't just dreaming about a better life. He was building one.

After taping the note cards around his life like little anchors, Sam stepped back toward the board again. Something tugged at him — not a missing task, not a forgotten goal, but something deeper.

His why. He uncapped the marker and wrote it across the bottom of the board, bigger than everything else:

Why? To be my best for my family, my work, and my friends.

He stood there for a moment, letting the words settle. This wasn't just a list anymore. It was a promise. Then he remembered something he'd heard years ago — that the more you write something down, the more you absorb it. The more you retain it. The more aware you become of what you're trying to do.

So he pulled out the note cards he bought and wrote his why again. Then again. Then again. Each card felt like a small anchor, something solid he could hold onto when the leaks started dripping again.

He taped one to the sun visor in his car — the place he'd see it every morning before work. He pinned another to the corkboard above his desk — a reminder in the middle of the chaos.

He set one on his nightstand — the last thing he'd see before bed and the first thing he'd see when he woke up. He didn't need perfection. He needed reminders. He needed intention.

He needed a why strong enough to pull him forward when everything else tried to pull him back. And now he had it — written, posted, visible, every-where he turned. For the first time in a long time, Sam felt aligned. Not just motivated. Not just hopeful. Aligned.

He wasn't just patching leaks anymore. He was building a life that could finally hold water. After placing the vision board on the wall, Sam stood there for a moment, taking it in. The goals. The why. The reminders. It all felt solid — but he knew himself too well.

A vision board could show him the path. But it couldn't make him walk it. So he pulled out his phone. One by one, he created alarms — not for waking up, but for becoming.

He titled the first one:

• Running — Start in 10 minutes

Then:

- Weight Training — Time to Move

Then:

- Poetry — 5 Minutes of Words

And finally:

- Guitar — 10 Minutes of Practice

He set each alarm for ten to fifteen minutes before he needed to begin the task — a built-in buffer, a nudge, a reminder that action doesn't happen by accident.

He stared at the list of alarms, each one a tiny promise. Vision boards were for vision. Alarms were for action. The board could show him who he wanted to be. But the alarms?

Those were the moments where he had to choose. He knew the truth now: Nothing takes root until you do the work. Nothing changes until you move. Nothing grows until you act.

He put his phone down, feeling something he hadn't felt in a long time — not motivation, not hype, but readiness. The kind that comes from structure. The kind that comes from intention.

The kind that comes from finally giving yourself the

tools to follow through. Sam wasn't just planning anymore. He was preparing. And preparation was the first real patch on the bucket.

Later that night, Sam sat on the edge of his bed, staring at the alarms he'd programmed. Running. Weight training. Poetry. Guitar. Four new habits. Four new leaks he was trying to patch at the same time.

He remembered hearing somewhere that if you do something over and over, eventually it becomes a habit. Eventually it sticks. Eventually it becomes automatic.

What he didn't know — what he couldn't know yet — was that every habit has its own timeline. Some take weeks. Some take months. Some take longer. And starting four at once meant he wasn't just building habits.

He was building patience. But he didn't see that yet. All he saw were the small chunks he'd carved out for himself:

- ten minutes of guitar
- five minutes of poetry
- a short run
- a simple strength session

Nothing overwhelming. Nothing heroic. Just enough to begin. He didn't realize that starting small wasn't a weakness. It was strategy. He didn't realize that slow beginnings weren't a delay. They were the foundation.

He didn't realize that every alarm he set was planting a seed — and each seed would sprout on its own timeline. All he knew was that he'd finally taken the first steps. All he knew was that he'd finally put structure around the life he wanted. All he knew was that he was showing up — even if the steps were tiny. And tiny was enough. Tiny was how things take root. Tiny was how buckets stop leaking. Tiny was how a new life begins.

The next morning, Sam's phone buzzed with the first alarm he'd programmed. Weight Training — Time to Move For a split second, the old version of him stirred — the one who would've hit snooze, rolled over, and promised himself he'd "start tomorrow." But not today. Today was different.

He got up, grabbed his gym bag, and drove to the gym before he could talk himself out of it. Chest and back day — simple, familiar, nothing overwhelming. He wasn't trying to be a hero. He was trying to begin.

He picked three exercises for each muscle group:

- light weights
- two sets
- small reps
- slow, controlled movement

Just enough to wake his body up. Just enough to avoid the kind of DOMS that would knock him out for two days and derail everything before it even started.

Thirty minutes. That's all it took. But when he finished — sweaty, steady, and standing a little taller — it felt like more than a workout. It felt like a promise kept.

He showered, changed, and headed into work with a quiet sense of accomplishment humming under his skin. Not pride. Not ego. Just... alignment. For the first time in a long time, he wasn't leaking. He was patching. One hole. One habit. One small win at a time. And as he walked into the building, he realized something simple and powerful: This is what it feels like when a new life begins — not with a dramatic moment, but with a single alarm you actually answer.

Sam walked into work feeling good — better than he had in months. His first alarm had gone off, and he'd actually answered it. He'd lifted. He'd moved. He'd kept a promise to himself.

But as he sat down at his desk and opened his lunch bag, something hit him like a slow-rolling truth. He'd forgotten about dieting. Not in a dramatic way. Not in a shameful way. Just... honestly.

He'd been so focused on running, weight training, poetry, and guitar — the four holes he could see — that he'd overlooked the one that leaked the most.

Food. Nutrition. The choices that shaped every other choice.

He sighed, not out of frustration, but out of recognition. This was another leak. A big one. And like everything else, it wasn't going to fix itself. He didn't need a perfect meal plan. He didn't need macros dialed in to the gram. He didn't need a 30-day challenge or a cleanse or a reset. He just needed a start. A small one.

So he opened his notes app and typed a single line: Diet Leak: Start with one simple rule — eat like the person I'm trying to become. No extremes. No punishments. No all-or-nothing. Just intention. Just awareness. Just one more patch on the bucket.

He closed the app, took a breath, and smiled to himself. He wasn't overwhelmed. He wasn't discouraged. He wasn't trying to fix everything at once. He was doing what he'd promised himself he would do: Start small. Start honest. Start now. And that was enough.

Sam finished his workday with a feeling he hadn't carried in a long time — accomplishment. Not the loud kind. Not the kind you brag about. Just a quiet, steady sense that he'd actually done what he said he would do.

On the drive home, he messaged one of his friends and told them what he was doing — the alarms, the board, the small steps, the plan. His friend responded almost immediately:

"Dude, that's awesome. I'm proud of you. Keep

going." It wasn't a long message. It didn't need to be. Support doesn't have to be loud to be real.

When Sam walked through the door at home, he found his family in the living room. He told them too — the board, the habits, the alarms, the why. They listened, nodded, and smiled.

"Yeah," one of them said, "we were wondering what the bulletin board was all about. We kind of figured it was something like that, but we didn't know the details."

Another added, "Whatever you need. We support you." Simple words. But they landed deep. Because for the first time in a long time, Sam wasn't hiding his goals. He wasn't keeping them quiet. He wasn't trying to change in the shadows. He was letting people in. And that mattered more than he realized.

Later that night, he got ready for bed — brushing his teeth, setting out his clothes, glancing at the note card on his nightstand with his why written across it. He felt tired, but it was a good tired. A purposeful tired.

Tomorrow would bring new alarms. New steps. New chances to patch the bucket. But tonight? Tonight he felt aligned. Supported. Ready.

He climbed into bed with the quiet confidence of someone who had finally taken the first real steps toward becoming who he wanted to be.

Sam went to bed that night and dreamed the night

away. Most of the dreams slipped through his fingers the moment he woke up — just flashes, fragments, feelings. But one dream stuck.

He saw a new version of himself. Not perfect. Not finished. Just... becoming. And he liked it. Before he could think too long about it, his phone buzzed. Run/Walk — 30 Minutes

He got up, pulled on his running clothes, and stepped outside into the cool morning air. The first few minutes felt good — better than expected — but soon enough he had to take a few walk breaks. He didn't beat himself up for it. He didn't quit. He just kept moving, alternating between running and walking until he looped back around to the house.

When he finished, he wasn't exhausted. He wasn't defeated. He was proud. He showered, got ready, and headed into work feeling accomplished — two days in a row.

Later that morning, another alarm buzzed. Guitar — 10 Minutes This time, he'd come prepared. He'd brought his guitar with him, tucked safely in the backseat. On his break, he slipped into an empty office, shut the door, and strummed through the chords he'd been practicing.

G.

D.

A.

Repeat. It wasn't pretty. It wasn't smooth. But it was progress. Afterward, he grabbed a coffee, took a quick bathroom break, and went back to work — a little lighter, a little more aligned.

When he got home that evening, another alarm chimed. Poetry — 5 Minutes He sat down at the kitchen table, opened his notebook, and brainstormed a few more ideas for the poem he'd abandoned years ago. Just a handful of words. A few images. A spark.

Then he helped his family make a healthy dinner — nothing extreme, nothing complicated, just a meal that matched the person he was trying to become. Nutrition wasn't a dramatic leak for him, but it was still a leak. And today, without even thinking too hard about it, he'd patched that one too.

By the time he got ready for bed, Sam felt something he hadn't felt in a long time. Not hype. Not motivation. Not pressure. Alignment.

He'd patched four holes today:

- Running
- Weight training (yesterday)
- Guitar
- Poetry
- And quietly, without fanfare — nutrition

He wasn't perfect. He wasn't finished. But he was

moving. And as he drifted off to sleep, he realized something simple and powerful:

This is how a bucket stops leaking — not with one big patch, but with small, steady repairs, day after day, until the water finally starts to rise.

That night, Sam fell asleep quickly — the good kind of tired, the kind that comes from a day lived with intention. And once again, he dreamed.

Most of the dreams blurred together, slipping away the moment he stirred. But one dream stayed sharp, vivid, almost too real to ignore.

He was back on the trail. Back at the wooden sign. Back at the bucket that had started everything. Only this time... the bucket wasn't rusted. It wasn't dented. It wasn't full of holes. It was whole. Perfect.

Hanging from the "**GENE WAS HERE**" sign like it had been waiting for him.

Sam walked closer. The bucket was filled to the brim with crystal-clear water — so clean it looked like it had been pulled straight from a mountain spring. A metal ladle rested inside, and beside it, on a small wooden shelf, sat a neat stack of cups.

Taped to the side of the bucket was a message written in thick black Sharpie: Drink one cup from the bucket every day and your dreams will come true. Sam stared at the words. Simple. Direct. Almost childlike. But the meaning hit him like a quiet revelation. One cup at a time. One day at a time. One hole at a time. That was the message.

That was the truth. He didn't need to fix everything at once. He didn't need to become the best version of himself overnight. He just needed to take one cup — one action — every day.

When he woke up, the dream stayed with him. Not the details, not the scenery, but the message. The clarity. The simplicity.

He got out of bed, stretched, and his phone buzzed. Weight Training — Time to Move He smiled. One cup. He went to the gym, lifted, and started his day.

And by the end of the week — seven days of alarms, seven days of small steps, seven days of patching leaks — he remembered the dream again. The bucket. The water. The Sharpie message.

So, he grabbed a marker, walked to his vision board, and wrote the words across the bottom: One cup at a time. One day at a time. One hole at a time. It wasn't just a reminder. It was a promise. A philosophy. A way forward. And for the first time in a long time, Sam felt like he wasn't just patching a bucket. He was filling it.

A few days later, after a long, draining evening, Sam crawled into bed and fell asleep almost instantly. He didn't even hear the alarm he'd set for one of his habits. It buzzed, vibrated, and eventually went silent. He missed it. Just like that — his first real setback.

He didn't know it yet, but the dream was coming. That night, he found himself back on the trail again. Back at the "GENE WAS HERE" sign. Back at the bucket. Only this time, something was different.

The bucket still hung from the sign, but now there was a tiny hole near the bottom — just one. Not the dozens from before. Just a single drip. Around the base of the sign, cups were scattered everywhere, blown across the ground like leaves after a storm. But one cup remained on the wooden shelf beside the bucket, standing upright. The ladle was still inside the water, steady and waiting.

And the message taped to the bucket had changed. Written in thick black Sharpie were new words: Setbacks happen. Keep drinking. Don't give up. One setback isn't failure. Sam stared at the message. It wasn't harsh. It wasn't judgmental. It wasn't disappointed. It was patient. It was kind. It was true.

He woke up with the dream still echoing in his mind. For a moment, he felt the old instinct — the one that whispered, "You messed up. You broke the streak. You failed."

But then he remembered the bucket. The cups. The single hole. The message. One setback isn't quitting. He got out of bed, stretched, and grabbed a Sharpie. He walked to his vision board and wrote the words across the bottom:

One setback doesn't equal quitting. He stepped back and looked at it — the board, the goals, the why, the messages from the dreams. It didn't feel like a failure. It felt like a lesson. He grabbed his phone, reset the alarm he'd missed, and started his day. Not perfect. Not flawless. But committed. And that was enough.

5

# REFLECTION, REPAIR, AND RESET

Sam goes on about his life for a few weeks and is really getting in the groove. He is patching holes and being consistent. Along the way he has had a few misses but keeps drinking the water. He looks back on his journey into this new normal.

When Sam fell asleep that night, it happened again. He was back on the trail. Back at the wooden sign. Back at the bucket. But this time, the air felt different — quieter, heavier, almost expectant.

The woods were still, like they were waiting for him to notice something he had missed before. He stepped closer to the bucket and looked inside. Instead of water, he saw his reflection. But it wasn't still. It was moving.

At first, the reflection looked like the version of himself he saw every morning — tired eyes, unfinished goals, a man still in progress. But as he watched, the surface of the water began to ripple, and the image started to change. He saw himself lacing up his shoes. Answering the alarm. Running... then walking... then running again. He watched himself pick up the guitar — awkward chords, buzzing strings, fingers fumbling for position.

He saw himself writing four lines of poetry... then crossing them out... then writing again. The reflection kept shifting. Every small win appeared in the water like scenes from a movie. Every alarm answered. Every workout completed. Every healthy meal chosen on the road.

But then he saw the leaks too. Missed alarms. Skipped runs. Moments where he chose comfort instead of growth. The bucket water dimmed slightly when those moments appeared — not dark, not ruined, just... imperfect.

Then he watched something new happen. He saw himself adjust. Reset the alarm. Shorten the workout instead of skipping it. Practice guitar for five minutes instead of ten. Write one line instead of five. The reflection brightened again. That was when he understood. Habits didn't fail. They required fine tuning.

. . .

THE IMAGE in the bucket began to change faster now — like time was speeding up. Weeks passed in seconds. Small patches layered over old leaks. His posture straightened. His face looked calmer. Stronger. Not perfect... but progressing.

He was becoming someone new — not a finished version, but a better one. Then the water stilled. And the reflection shifted one last time. Sam saw himself sitting at a campfire party deep in the woods. Lanterns hung from tree branches. Runners sat in folding chairs. Laughter echoed through the night air.

AND THERE HE WAS — guitar in hand. Playing. Not perfectly. But confidently. People clapped along as he strummed, the same chords that once felt impossible now flowing naturally beneath his fingers.

HE SMILED IN THE REFLECTION — relaxed, proud, alive in a way he hadn't felt in years. It was a glimpse into the future. A reward for the patches. A vision of who he was becoming. Sam leaned closer to the bucket, studying the image, trying to hold onto it.

. . .

AND THAT WAS when it happened. From somewhere high in the trees above, a pawpaw fruit dropped straight into the bucket. SPLASH. Water exploded upward, drenching his face.

Sam jerked awake in bed, heart racing, breath sharp — the feeling of cold water still lingering on his skin. He sat up slowly, letting the dream settle into his mind. Reflection. Adjustment. Fine tuning.

He didn't need to become perfect. He just needed to keep refining the patches. One habit at a time. One adjustment at a time. One better version of himself at a time.

Sam woke up slowly, the dream still clinging to him like early morning fog. For a moment he lay still, replaying it — the reflection, the habits unfolding, the small leaks, the adjustments, the glimpse of who he was becoming.

Before the details could slip away, he grabbed his notebook and began writing everything he could remember. The bucket.The reflection changing. The small wins. The leaks that dimmed the water.

The adjustments that brightened it again. The future glimpse by the fire. The splash of the pawpaw fruit. He wrote until his thoughts felt emptied onto the page.

Then he stood and walked to the hallway where his vision board hung. Start. Now. Future Self. He studied it carefully. Some areas were filling in. Some habits were steady. But there were still holes. Smaller than before — but there.

He stepped closer. Poetry. Weight Training. Those were the two that needed more consistency. Not abandonment. Not failure. Just fine tuning. He uncapped a marker and circled them gently on the board. Not as a reprimand. As a reminder.

He stood back and breathed. This timeline, he realized, was just a timeline. It wasn't fixed. It wasn't a deadline. It wasn't a race. Growth didn't have to come all at once. Perfection wasn't required. Consistency mattered more than intensity. Leaks were going to be there. That was life.

Sometimes you just needed a little plumber's tape. Sometimes a little extra glue. He smiled at the thought. Then he walked to the bathroom mirror. For a moment, he studied his reflection. No shifting water. Just him. But something was different. His shoulders were back. His eyes were steady.

There was a quiet confidence there — not because everything was perfect, but because he was no longer running from the work. He liked what he saw. That night, he went to bed feeling satisfied. Not finished. Not flawless. Satisfied. And he dreamed again.

The bucket hung from the wooden sign, swaying

gently in the night breeze. It rocked back and forth, back and forth — but the water inside didn't spill.

It held. Strong. Steady. At the very bottom, where the old leaks once lived, a tiny smile-shaped shimmer glowed in the metal — not a crack, not a drip. Just a reminder of where he'd been. With each sway of the bucket, the wind moved through the trees. And in that wind, he thought he heard something soft.

Continue on. Whichever way the wind blows your path. The bucket kept swinging. The water kept holding. And when he woke the next morning, he felt ready. Not for perfection. But for the next cup.

**6**

---

## LIVING WITH INTENTION

Sam woke up from the dream with the words still echoing in his mind — Continue on.

Before the meaning could slip away, he grabbed his notebook and wrote the phrase down, underlining it once, then twice. It felt simple, but it carried weight.

He walked into the hallway and stopped in front of his vision board. Start. Now. Future Self. The words stared back at him like a quiet promise. He didn't add anything. He didn't erase anything. He just stood there, letting the message settle.

Then he continued on. He moved through his day answering every alarm as it chimed — run, lift, guitar, poetry, nutrition. Not perfectly, not dramatically, just consistently. One patch at a time. One cup at a time. One small act of becoming at a time.

Days turned into weeks, and the rhythm became natural. The alarms stopped feeling like interruptions and started feeling unnecessary. One morning, without ceremony, he opened his phone and turned them all off.

He didn't need them anymore. He knew what to do. He knew who he was becoming. And he continued on — steady, focused, not missing a beat.

For months, Sam hit every note of his new life with steady rhythm. He wrote the lines. He lifted the weight. He ate the meals he once avoided. He ran the miles he used to dread. And it showed.

He looked in the mirror and actually liked what he saw — not just the muscle, not just the leanness, but the posture, the steadiness, the way his eyes held a quiet confidence. His guitar playing had taken off too; he could play half the song he'd chosen, not perfectly, but proudly. He told his friends and family about his progress, and they noticed. Everyone noticed.

People commented on the way he carried himself — the way he walked into a room with energy that seemed to bounce off him. Compliments came from everywhere: his fitness, his discipline, the calluses forming on his fingertips, the poems that flowed cleanly onto the page. His runs felt effortless now. His weight training had leveled up — heavy sets, long sessions, real strength. Five to six miles at a time felt normal.

His guitar instructor even graduated him to the next teacher, the one who specialized in rhythm. His brainstorming notebook was filled cover to cover; he had to buy a new one.

Life was good. Life was full. Life was working. He went to bed each night satisfied and slept deeply. He hadn't dreamed in a while — not the bucket dreams, not the whispers, not the visions. Just rest. But the next morning, life shifted.

Work got harder. People were calling off, and Sam picked up the slack. The kids were in three or four sports between them, which meant he had to be in multiple places at once. Practices, games, carpools, late nights, early mornings — the schedule tightened around him.

Even with all of that, he held the line. He kept the habits. He kept the rhythm. But for the first time in months... he felt a flicker of worry. Not because he was slipping — but because he could feel how easy it would be to slip.

That night, after the long day's journey, Sam drifted into sleep expecting the familiar woods — the bucket hanging steady from the wooden sign, the quiet sway, the calm water.

But this time, something was wrong. The bucket

wasn't hanging at all. It lay on its side in the dirt, tipped over, water spilled into a dark puddle that soaked into the leaves. The air felt heavier, colder — not threatening, just honest. Sam stepped closer and looked down into the puddle.

His reflection stared back at him, but it wasn't the confident version he'd seen before. He watched himself forgetting to practice the guitar. Missing a few runs. Choosing comfort over consistency. Little slips. Little leaks.

The kind that don't break a person — but slowly drain them. Sam knelt, lifted the bucket with both hands, and set it upright again. The metal felt colder than usual, like it remembered the fall. As he steadied it, a soft wind moved through the trees, carrying a voice he had heard before — gentle, steady, familiar.

Walk the way you should always walk. With your head held high. Setbacks only make you stronger. The bucket settled. The woods grew still. And Sam felt something shift inside him — not shame, not fear, but resolve. He had spilled some water. So what. He knew how to refill it.

7

———————

# WHEN THE BUCKET LEAKS AGAIN

When he woke the next morning, he wasn't discouraged. He was ready. He was ready to start the day. He pulled on his workout clothes, packed his lunch, laid out his work outfit, and stepped outside with that quiet confidence he'd earned over months of consistency.

The morning air felt good. The plan was solid. Everything was in motion. Then he turned the key. Nothing. A hollow click. A dead dashboard. Silence.

Sam tried again. Same result. He popped the hood, checked the cables, jogged back inside, and spent the next thirty or forty minutes tearing through the garage looking for the battery charger he hadn't touched in years. By the time he found it, hooked it up, and coaxed the engine back to life, the window for his workout had evaporated.

He sat in the driver's seat for a moment, hands on the wheel, breathing through the frustration. The old version of him would've let this ruin the whole day. Maybe the whole week. But now?

In the back of his mind, he was already adjusting. Already shifting. Already planning. I'll get it in tonight, he thought. I'll make it work. The setback stung, but it didn't break him.

Not yet. Sam moved through his morning at work with the same steady rhythm he'd built over the past few months. No alarms. No buzzes. Just instinct — the quiet knowing of when it was time to shift gears.

Late morning rolled around, and he felt it — that familiar internal cue, the one that used to come from his phone but now lived in his bones. Guitar time.

He reached for the case he always kept in the back seat. But the moment his hand touched empty air, he remembered. The dead car. The scramble. The charger. The rush out the door. In all of that chaos, he'd forgotten to load the guitar.

For a second, he felt the tiniest drop in his chest — not panic, not shame, just that soft dang it that comes when a rhythm stutters. But he caught it quickly, breathed, and adjusted.

It's alright, he thought. Today I'll brainstorm.

Tomorrow I'll bring the guitar. It wasn't a failure. It wasn't even a slip. It was just life being life. And Sam did what he'd learned to do — he pivoted, calmly, confidently, without losing the thread.

Sam made it through the workday, steady but stretched. He still felt that internal cue — the one that used to come from alarms — telling him it was time to train. He headed toward the gym, determined to salvage what he could of the day.

He only had time for half a workout before family duties pulled him in another direction, but half was better than none. He grabbed his keys, walked to the car, and— Nothing. The battery was dead again.

He stared at the dashboard in disbelief, a tired laugh slipping out. Twice in one day. Twice in one morning. Twice in one life that was already full. He got the hood open, hooked up the charger, coaxed the engine back to life, and drove his family where they needed to go. Then he headed straight to the auto parts store, hoping for a quick fix.

The test confirmed what he already suspected: the battery was done. He bought a new one. Had it replaced. Watched the daylight fade while the minutes slipped away.

By the time everything was finished, the window for his workout had closed completely. There was no salvaging it. No adjusting. No squeezing it in.

Just a long, full day that had taken more than it gave.

Sam drove home, tired in a way that wasn't physical. He finished out the evening with what little energy he had left, then finally crawled into bed. He didn't beat himself up. He didn't spiral.

He didn't quit. But as he drifted toward sleep, he felt it — that quiet awareness that today had taken a cup of water from the bucket. And tomorrow would ask for more.

Sam woke up the next morning determined to reset the rhythm. He packed his lunch, grabbed his gym bag, and headed out early. This time, the car started. This time, he made it to the gym. And when he finally got his workout in, it felt good — like reclaiming a piece of himself.

He went into work feeling steadier, ready to keep the day on track. And when the moment came — that internal cue he'd learned to trust — he reached for his guitar out of habit. Except he'd forgotten it again.

He closed his eyes for a second, exhaled, and let the frustration pass through him instead of sticking. No big deal, he told himself. I'll brainstorm today. Poetry counts. Creativity counts. I'll bring the guitar tomorrow.

He pivoted, just like before. But later that afternoon, the team was called into a meeting. Sam sat down expecting the usual updates, the usual reminders, the usual shuffle of tasks.

Instead, he learned that one of his coworkers had decided to leave — and leadership wasn't planning to replace them. The workload wasn't being redistributed across the team. It was being handed directly to him.

Sam felt the weight of it settle on his shoulders. Not crushing, not impossible, but heavy — the kind of heavy that doesn't hit all at once. The kind that accumulates. The kind that slowly drains the bucket if you're not careful.

He nodded, took the notes, accepted the new responsibilities. He didn't complain. He didn't push back. He just absorbed it, the way he always had. But inside, he felt it — that quiet shift. That tightening.

That sense that life was beginning to ask more of him than he had room to give. And for the first time, he wondered how long he could keep all the pieces moving.

The next morning, Sam tried again to steady himself. He made it to work on time, settled into his routine, and when the moment came to write poetry, he opened his notebook like he always did.

But as he shifted in his chair, his elbow clipped his coffee cup. It tipped. It spilled. A wave of dark liquid rushed across the page. He watched helplessly as the ink bled, the words blurred, and the pages he'd filled with weeks of ideas soaked through. His notebook — the one he'd carried everywhere — was ruined. All that progress... gone, he thought.

He closed the cover gently, set it aside, and lowered his head into his hands. Not in defeat — just in exhaustion. He sat there for a few minutes, breathing, thinking about life, about the week he'd had, about how quickly things could slip.

The rest of the week followed the same pattern — small setbacks, long days, heavy workloads, missed cues, and the quiet pressure of trying to hold everything together. Nothing catastrophic. Nothing dramatic. Just life tightening around him, inch by inch.

Then Friday came, and with it something that looked like good news. A pizza party at work — a celebration for all the hard work the team had put in over the last few months. Tables full of boxes, the smell filling the room, everyone laughing and relaxing for the first time all week.

Sam looked at the pizza. Then he thought about the week he'd just survived. The dead battery. The forgotten guitar. The spilled notebook. The extra workload. The exhaustion. And something in him cracked. He didn't take one slice. He didn't take two.

He ate emotionally — slice after slice — not because he was hungry, but because he was tired. Because he was stretched thin. Because he needed comfort, and this was the closest thing in reach. It wasn't a failure. It wasn't weakness. It was a human moment at the end of a long, heavy week. And Sam felt it — the bucket leaking again.

The weekend arrived, and Sam felt it the moment he opened his eyes — the heaviness, the mental fog, the emotional fatigue from the week that had taken more than it gave. He skipped the gym without even arguing with himself. He postponed the guitar. He avoided the vision board entirely.

He wasn't angry. He wasn't dramatic. He was just tired. He ordered takeout on Saturday. Then again on Sunday. He vegged out on the couch, drifting between rest, food, thoughts, family time, and messages with friends — the two things that still felt steady, still felt good, still felt like they weren't slipping through his fingers.

He didn't do much else. And honestly, he didn't have much else to give. By Sunday night, he crawled into bed feeling drained in a way that wasn't physical. He hadn't dreamed in months — not since the bucket had warned him. But that night, something stirred.

He found himself back in the woods. The bucket was there, riddled with holes again — but this time, it had grown legs. Before Sam could react, it took off running through the trees, water spraying everywhere, splashing wildly as it leaked from every patch he'd ever made. Sam chased it, branches whipping past him, the sound of dripping water echoing like a heartbeat.

By the time he caught it, the bucket was empty. Completely drained. He bent down, breathless, and lifted it. Inside, instead of water, he found a contract and a pen. The paper was crisp, the ink bold, the message unmistakable:

A vow to keep patching. Not perfectly. But persistently. Sam pulled the contract and pen from the bucket and signed it right there in the dream — a commitment to lifelong patching, to showing up even when he slipped, to choosing persistence over perfection.

When he woke Monday morning, the dream clung to him like morning fog. He walked straight to his vision board, wrote the commitment in bold letters, and signed it. Then he printed a physical copy, signed that too, sealed it in an envelope, and taped it behind the whiteboard — hidden, but present. A promise only he knew about. A vow to continue on.

8

———

# RECOMMITMENT &
# SYSTEM BUILDING

Sam woke up from the dream slowly, the images still clinging to him. He wasn't fired up or overflowing with motivation — he was reflective. Quiet. Honest with himself.

He realized something he had never considered before: Patching leaks wasn't enough, if he kept reopening them. He needed to be proactive. He needed to reinforce the bucket, not just repair it.

On Monday, after work, Sam drove to the guitar store. He bought several packs of strings and signed up for a quick lesson on how to replace them himself. It wasn't glamorous, but it was practical — one less leak waiting to happen. When he finished, he went home, ate dinner with his family, and went to bed.

The next day, he bought a waterproof notebook and

a fresh Sharpie — something durable, something that could survive a spill. That evening, he set up a weekly "walk-around check" for his car. Every Saturday morning, he'd spend a few minutes checking the battery and cables. A tiny habit. A preventative patch.

The day after that, he ordered meal-prep containers and looked up simple recipes he could make ahead of time. He scheduled his workouts. He laid out his clothes. He prepared for the next morning.

It wasn't a dramatic comeback. It was a steady one. And over the next few weeks, Sam found his rhythm again. Slowly at first, then naturally. The workouts returned. The guitar returned. The writing returned. The confidence returned. He was patching holes again — but this time, with intention.

One evening, feeling stronger, he decided to drive out to the night-race course. He wanted to see the trail again, to reconnect with the place where everything had started. He walked through the woods until he reached the old wooden sign.

"Gene was here." And hanging from it — the bucket. But this time, when Sam looked at it, he didn't see leaks. He saw lessons. Every hole represented something he had learned. Every patch represented growth. Every scar represented progress. He finally understood.

He looked past the bucket and noticed an old barn down the hill — the same barn his uncle used to weld in. The same place where sparks flew late into the night. Now Gene welded there, building things, repairing things, shaping metal into purpose.

Sam walked toward it, carrying the bucket. Tools were scattered in the grass nearby, as if waiting for him. He unhooked the gate, stepped inside, and saw the welder still warm.

He thought to himself: Gene is either gone... or preparing to leave. Sam placed the bucket on the bench. He welded the handle joints. The base seams. The high-pressure leak zones. He reinforced the places that had always given him trouble.

As he finished, Gene appeared in the doorway. He didn't speak. He didn't need to. He looked at the bucket, noticed the missing pamphlet, and understood that Sam had taken the torch — literally and symbolically. Gene nodded once, quietly, and walked away.

Sam now had the tools he needed. He picked up the bucket and examined it. Welded seams. Strong joints. Reinforced structure. He peeled off one old patch — and nothing happened. No gush of water. No collapse. The seams held.

So he drilled one intentional hole and attached a small spout. Water flowed out slowly, steadily, in a controlled stream. A release. Not a leak.

He hung the bucket back on the sign. It looked different now — patched, welded, strengthened, and equipped with a spout. A bucket built for living, not surviving.

Sam walked back to his car, drove home, and fell into bed. His body was exhausted, but his mind was calm. For the first time in a long time, he wasn't stressed. He wasn't overwhelmed. He was at peace.

That night, he dreamed again. He stood at the sign, but it was dawn now — not dusk. The light was soft. The air was still. The bucket hung quietly, no drips, the water inside calm and clear.

He looked around and saw dozens of buckets hanging from the trees. Some rusted. Some patched. Some welded. Some empty. Some overflowing.

No explanations. No labels. Just truth. Everyone was carrying something. Everyone was patching something. Everyone struggled — not just him. Gene appeared behind the barn, watching. He didn't speak, but Sam heard the words anyway: "You figured it out."

Sam walked to his bucket and ran his fingers along the welded seams. He touched the spout he had created. Water began to flow again — not spilling, not wasting, but pouring downhill in a gentle stream. He followed it.

The water flowed into small buckets below, filling them slowly, steadily, without draining his own. He understood. His strength wasn't just for him anymore. It was meant to support others — without emptying himself.

He looked back into the bucket and saw the pamphlet again. But it wasn't the same. It was filled with his handwriting now — notes, reflections, lessons from his journey. The message was changing because he had changed.

He looked up. All the buckets swayed in the wind. The water levels shifted, but held. Sam stepped toward his bucket calmly. No rush. No panic. Just understanding.

## THE OCTOBER RACE (THE TEST)

Today was the day. The night race. Sam woke up buzzing with nervous energy — the good kind, the electric kind. He drove to the store to buy a headlamp, but only one remained on the shelf. The other runners must've grabbed the rest, he thought, smiling. This one was meant for him.

Back home, he plugged in his Garmin, loaded fresh batteries into the headlamp, and pulled out a small flashlight to carry in his hand. He laid out his outfit, his shoes, his water, and two energy gels. The race wouldn't start until dark, which meant he had all day to sit with the nerves.

Excited nerves. Earned nerves. To settle himself, he opened his poem book and read his Darkness Falls poem once through. Then he tuned his guitar, played a few soft chords, and slid it gently into its case.

Hours later, his family drove with him to the Boy Scout camp. The parking lot buzzed with life — headlights, laughter, gravel crunching under hundreds of feet. He checked in, pinned his bib to his shirt, and watched volunteers build a fire near the lake beside the tiki poles.

Two hundred runners showed up. Glowsticks lit the trees like fireflies. Excitement hummed in the air. The race director called everyone to the starting line. "Two rules," he said. "Don't blind anyone with your light. And if you pass, yell loud enough so they know you're coming."

That was it. A cannon fired. And Sam took off. Headlamps bobbed. Flashlights flickered. Footsteps pounded. Breathing filled the night. By mile four, the hill hit him hard. His legs burned. His lungs tightened. But he hadn't walked yet — and he was out front, alone, the woods swallowing the sound behind him.

The bucket was gone. And for the first time, he thought: I don't need the bucket right now. He pushed harder — not from hype, not from adrenaline, but from structure. From the welds he'd made. From the patches he'd reinforced. From the calm water inside him that no longer spilled with every stumble.

With each footstep, he thought of the seams holding. With each breath, he felt the steadiness he'd built. Nothing was leaking. Ahead, he heard cheering. Saw the fire glowing. Smelled the soup, the cider, the s'mores. He sprinted the final stretch.

Seven miles. Thirty-eight minutes. First place over-all. A volunteer handed him a hand-carved wooden medal — one of a kind, earned, not bought. And then he saw it. Hanging by the chute: Gene was here. And the bucket. A ladle. Cups.

A sign that read: Take a drink. Be refreshed. Fill your cup. Every runner who finished took a drink from the bucket. It was the best water anyone had tasted in a long time. Sam stepped forward, lifted the ladle, and drank deeply.

Sam sat on a wooden log near the fire, the glow reflecting off the lake as the last of the adrenaline faded from his body. His breathing slowed. His mind settled. And then, without forcing it, the words came to him.

He opened his notebook and wrote the poem he had abandoned years ago. Line after line flowed out of him until it was finally complete. When he finished, he read it once, then again, and closed the notebook gently. A leak patched. A circle closed.

He stood and walked toward the fire where runners, families, volunteers, and friends were gathered in a wide circle. Glowsticks flickered. People laughed. Someone passed around hot cider. The night felt alive.

Sam took out his guitar. The crowd quieted as he strummed the first chords of the song he had practiced just for this moment. His voice carried across the circle, warm and steady. A few people began to sing along, then more, until the whole group was wrapped in the sound of music and firelight.

When he finished, the crowd erupted in cheers. "One more!" someone shouted. Sam smiled. "Alright... one more." He played a simple, spooky little tune that matched the October woods, and he sang the poem he had just written:

Dust off your headlamps and follow the glow!

It's dark and spooky in the woods just so you know!

Lace up your trail shoes nice and tight!

Be cautious and vigilant and watch for the fright!

Into the woods you will eventually go!

Just follow the light and go with the flow!

Up and down the hills you will flee!

Turn off your lights just for a second to see!

Finish up at the lake and warm up by the fire!

But not too close so you don't perspire!

Enjoy refreshments until the night ends!

Stick around and make some new friends!

Remember the fun you had in the twilight!

You're now a trail runner that goes spook in the night! When the last note faded, the crowd cheered again — louder this time, fuller, as if they understood what this moment meant for him. Sam stayed until the fire burned low. Then he packed up, hugged his family, and headed home.

The next morning, he returned to the hill where he had first found the bucket. He carried it with him — cleaned, welded, patched, strengthened — and inside he placed fresh pamphlets for whoever needed them next.

He hung the bucket back on the sign. Under the old carving that read "GENE WAS HERE," he added a new one:

"Sam Was Here." He stepped back, took a breath, and smiled. His bucket held water now. And it always would.

# EPILOGUE — THE FINAL POEM

Sam's journey wasn't about perfection.

It was about persistence — patching the leaks, reinforcing the seams, and learning to pour without emptying himself.

And in the end, the poem he once abandoned became the final proof that he had changed.

Dust off your headlamps and follow the glow!

It's dark and spooky in the woods just so you know!

Lace up your trail shoes nice and tight!

Be cautious and vigilant and watch for the fright!

Into the woods you will eventually go!

Just follow the light and go with the flow!

Up and down the hills you will flee!

Turn off your lights just for a second to see!

Finish up at the lake and warm up by the fire!

But not too close so you don't perspire!

Enjoy refreshments until the night ends!

Stick around and make some new friends!

Remember the fun you had in the twilight!

You're now a trail runner that goes spook in the night!

# CONCLUSION — A BUCKET THAT HOLDS WATER

We all carry a bucket with holes.

Some leaks we ignore. Some we hide. Some drain us dry. Sam didn't change by becoming someone new. He changed by finally admitting where the water was going. That's the whole point. Patch one leak. Then another. Then another. Not perfectly — just honestly. He welded the weak spots. Reinforced the seams. Stopped pouring everything out.

And slowly, the bucket started holding water. Yours will too. You don't need a new life. You don't need a perfect plan. You don't need to wait for Monday. You just need to start patching. One leak. One step. One moment of truth. And when your bucket finally holds — even a little — you'll understand what Sam learned:

You were never meant to be perfect. You were meant to persist. Patch your bucket. Let the water rise. Continue on.

# AUTHOR'S NOTE

This story grew out of real places and real moments from my life — some I expected, and some that showed up out of nowhere and made me laugh in the middle of a race.

The sign in this book is real. It hangs behind my cousin Gene's childhood home. I had no idea it existed. I didn't know anyone had carved "Gene was here" into a wooden board.

The first time I ever saw it was during the KT 50k, running with my friend Chris Leslie. We were tired, muddy, and questioning all our life choices when we came around a bend and — boom — there's my cousin's name carved into a sign like he'd been out there marking territory.

I actually laughed out loud. Chris looked at me like I'd finally snapped. But honestly, what are the odds? You're deep in the woods, half-broken, and suddenly your cousin's name is staring at you like he's been waiting there the whole time. I didn't plan to use it in a story. It just stuck with me, the way certain symbols do when they refuse to leave you alone.

The bucket, though — that part is fiction. But the leaks and patches? Those are real. Those are mine. Sam's name is real too. His initials — S.A.M. — come from my best friend, Scott Alan Murphy. I didn't set out to name the character after him. It just happened, the way things tend to when you're writing from the gut instead of the outline.

The guitar scene is real. It happened at my brother Joey's house years ago. I didn't expect it to end up in a book, but it fit — another unfinished thread that finally found a home.

None of these details were planned. They revealed themselves as I wrote, like the story already knew what it wanted and I was just trying to keep up.

This book is fiction, but the symbols are mine. The sign. The leaks. The patches. The places. The people. The moments that shaped me long before I ever put them on the page. If this parable feels real, it's because it is.

It came from the life I've lived — the struggles, the

restarts, the unfinished things, and the quiet decision to finally patch the leaks instead of pretending they weren't there. My hope is simple: that somewhere in these pages, you recognize a piece of your own bucket... and find the courage to patch it.

www.ingramcontent.com/pod-product-compliance
Lightning Source LLC
Chambersburg PA
CBHW071459130726
47997CB00006B/2403